MY FIRST
OCEAN
ATLAS

Illustrated by Paul Daviz
Written by Catherine Ard

EARTHAWARE
KIDS

Illustrated by Paul Daviz
Written by Catherine Ard
Ocean Consultant: Dr. David Ferrier, University of St. Andrews

weldon**owen**

Published by EarthAware Kids
Created by Weldon Owen Children's Books
A subsidiary of Insight International, LP.

PO Box 3088
San Rafael, CA 94912
www.insighteditions.com

Weldon Owen Children's Books
Senior Editor: Pauline Savage
Senior Designer: Emma Randall

Insight Editions
Publisher: Raoul Goff
Senior Production Manager: Greg Steffen

ISBN: 979-8-88674-038-7

Printed in China
First printing July, 2024

DRM0724

10 9 8 7 6 5 4 3 2 1

FSC
www.fsc.org
MIX
Paper | Supporting
responsible forestry
FSC® C188448

CONTENTS

WELCOME TO THE OCEAN!

If you gaze out at the ocean from the shore, all you see is miles of wavy water. From the surface, the ocean looks empty, but underneath it is bursting with life. Here you'll find a dazzling array of creatures, from whales as big as a bus to shrimp the size of a pea.

   Some parts of the ocean are warm and shallow, and brim with colorful fish. Other parts are deep, dark, and cold, and strange creatures flash and glow. Dive below the surface and discover the amazing world of the ocean!

Humpback whale fluke

TOP HUNTERS

Lots of ocean creatures are predators—they hunt other creatures. Sharks can sniff out prey from miles away.

Blacktip reef shark

Moorish idols

OCEAN DRIFTERS

Not all ocean creatures are good swimmers. Seahorses are carried by the currents.

Seahorse

SPOT IT! Can you see a fish with fins that look like hands?

SKY SPY

Seabirds soar over the ocean looking for food. They swoop down and scoop up their catch.

Albatross

FAST SWIMMERS

Many fish have smooth, torpedo-shaped bodies that help them swim speedily. The sailfish is the fastest swimmer in the ocean.

Sailfish

WARM COAT

Ocean creatures must be able to survive in chilly seawater. The sea otter's thick, waterproof fur helps it to stay warm.

Sea otter

Cuckoo wrasse

COLOR CHANGE

Some creatures, such as the giant cuttlefish, can change color. They do this to send messages to others or to hide in their surroundings.

Giant cuttlefish

Red handfish

Which creature likes to float on the surface of the water?

Dog whelks

Limpets

Limpets

Beadlet anemone

LONG ARMS

The brittlestar has long, delicate arms. It stretches them out to catch tiny bits of food in the water.

Brittlestar

Montagu's blenny

AIR BREATHER

The Montagu's blenny can survive out of water. At low tide, it breathes air while sheltering under rocks and seaweed.

Hermit crab

Beadlet anemone

SEA STINGERS

Under the water, the beadlet anemone traps food with its stinging tentacles. When it is above water, the anemone pulls its tentacles in.

TIDE POOL

Twice a day, the ocean rises before falling back again. Slowly, the water comes in and creeps up over the shore until it reaches high tide. When the tide goes out, little pools of seawater are left in rocky dips and cracks.

A tide pool is like a miniature ocean world. Crabs hide in the seaweed and little fish dart to and fro between crevices. Limpets, whelks, and anemones cling to rocks so that they don't get swept away. Some fish are born here before spending the rest of their lives in the open seas.

SPOT IT! Can you see a baby shark inside a mermaid's purse?

Gut weed

Mermaid's purse

FISHY PURSE

Sharks lay their eggs inside a leathery case called a mermaid's purse. The baby shark hatches, then swims away as soon as it is high tide.

Sea star

PIPEFISH PARENT

A sheltered pool is a good place to bring up young. For pipefish, it's the male that cares for the female's eggs, carrying them in a groove on his tummy.

STUCK FAST

Some of the little rock goby fins are joined together to form a sucker. The fish sticks to rocks to stop itself from being swept out to sea.

Pipefish

Serrated wrack seaweed

Rock goby

BRIGHT EYES

The velvet swimming crab has bright red beady eyes. Its body is covered in small hairs that are soft to the touch.

Velvet swimming crab

How many anemones can you count? Which creatures have five arms?

FLOODED FOREST

On tropical shores, thick mangrove forests grow along the water's edge. As the tide comes in and out, they are first flooded, then left high and dry. At low tide, mangrove trees look like they are standing on stilts because their long roots raise them up above the ground.

When the tangled tree roots are below the water, they make a good place for small creatures to hide. Big hunters visit the mangrove forest to find food. Many of the creatures here spend time both in the water and on land.

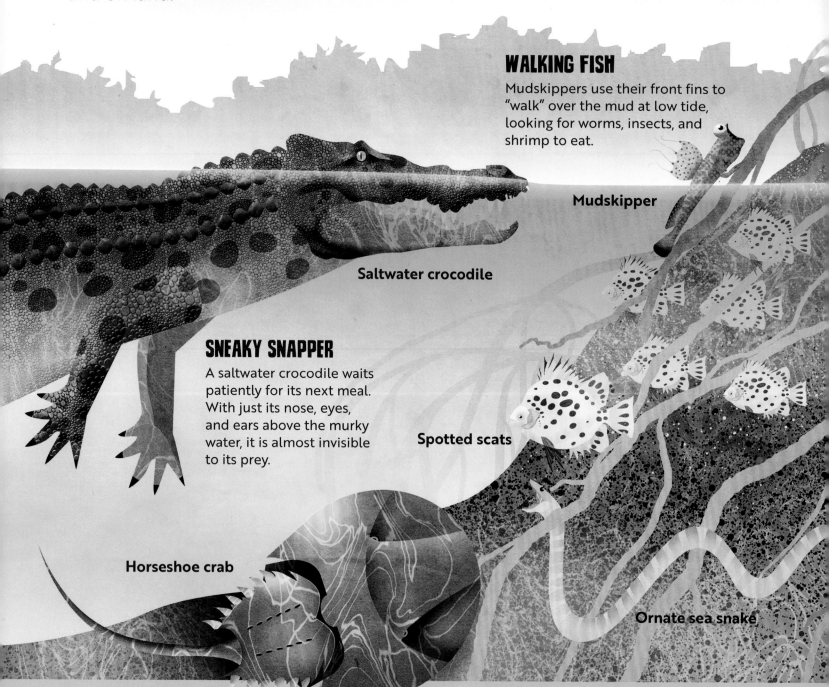

WALKING FISH

Mudskippers use their front fins to "walk" over the mud at low tide, looking for worms, insects, and shrimp to eat.

Mudskipper

Saltwater crocodile

SNEAKY SNAPPER

A saltwater crocodile waits patiently for its next meal. With just its nose, eyes, and ears above the murky water, it is almost invisible to its prey.

Spotted scats

Horseshoe crab

Ornate sea snake

SPOT IT! Can you see a creature that is shaped like a horseshoe?

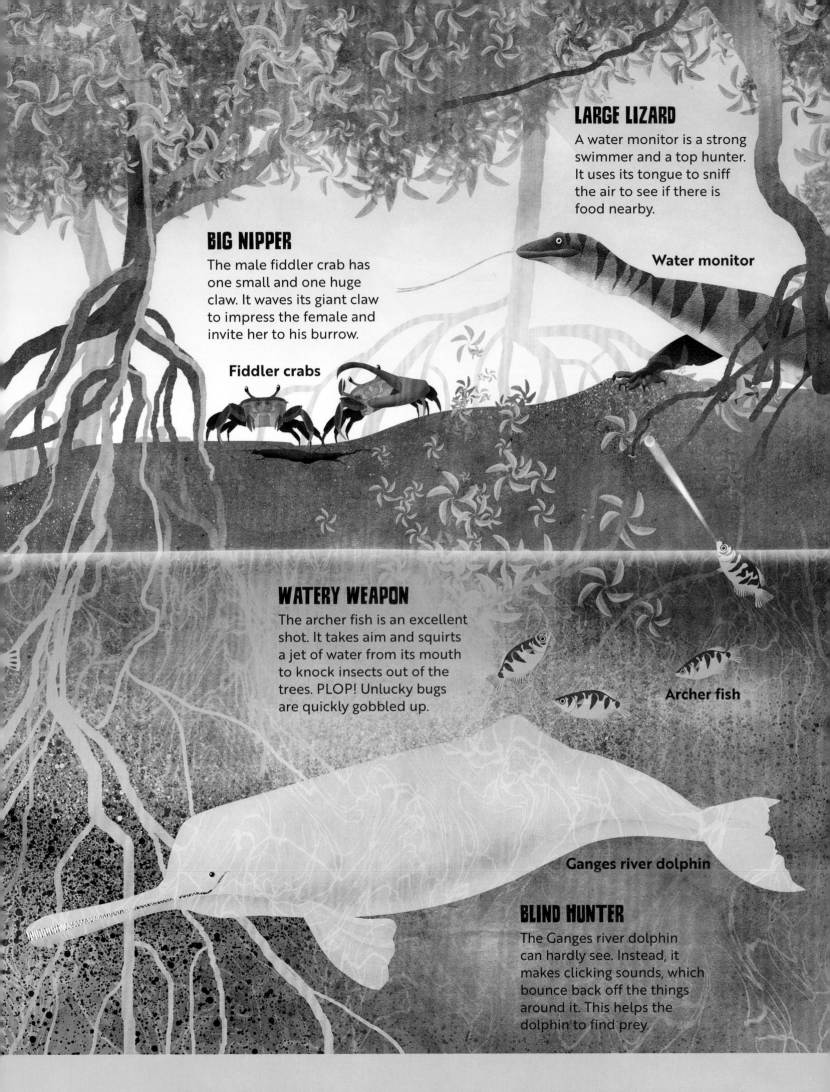

LARGE LIZARD

A water monitor is a strong swimmer and a top hunter. It uses its tongue to sniff the air to see if there is food nearby.

Water monitor

BIG NIPPER

The male fiddler crab has one small and one huge claw. It waves its giant claw to impress the female and invite her to his burrow.

Fiddler crabs

WATERY WEAPON

The archer fish is an excellent shot. It takes aim and squirts a jet of water from its mouth to knock insects out of the trees. PLOP! Unlucky bugs are quickly gobbled up.

Archer fish

Ganges river dolphin

BLIND HUNTER

The Ganges river dolphin can hardly see. Instead, it makes clicking sounds, which bounce back off the things around it. This helps the dolphin to find prey.

Snakes, crocodiles, and lizards are all reptiles—how many reptiles can you spot?

SEAGRASS SAFARI

All around the world, from icy oceans to warm tropical seas, lush green meadows grow in shallow waters. They are full of underwater plants called seagrass. The long blades of grass gently swoosh and sway with the motion of the ocean.

Big ocean creatures visit to graze on the juicy grasses and small ones make their homes between the plants. Many fish lay their eggs here. It's a safe place for their young to grow up.

GRACEFUL GLIDER

A southern eagle ray slowly flaps its wide fins to glide over the meadow. It has its babies here in spring and summer.

Southern eagle ray

HEALTHY APPETITE

Green turtles munch through a pound of seagrass each day. That's like eating 25 helpings of peas!

Green turtle

Blue swimmer crab

Leafy sea dragon

SPOT IT! Which creature looks like a piece of seaweed?

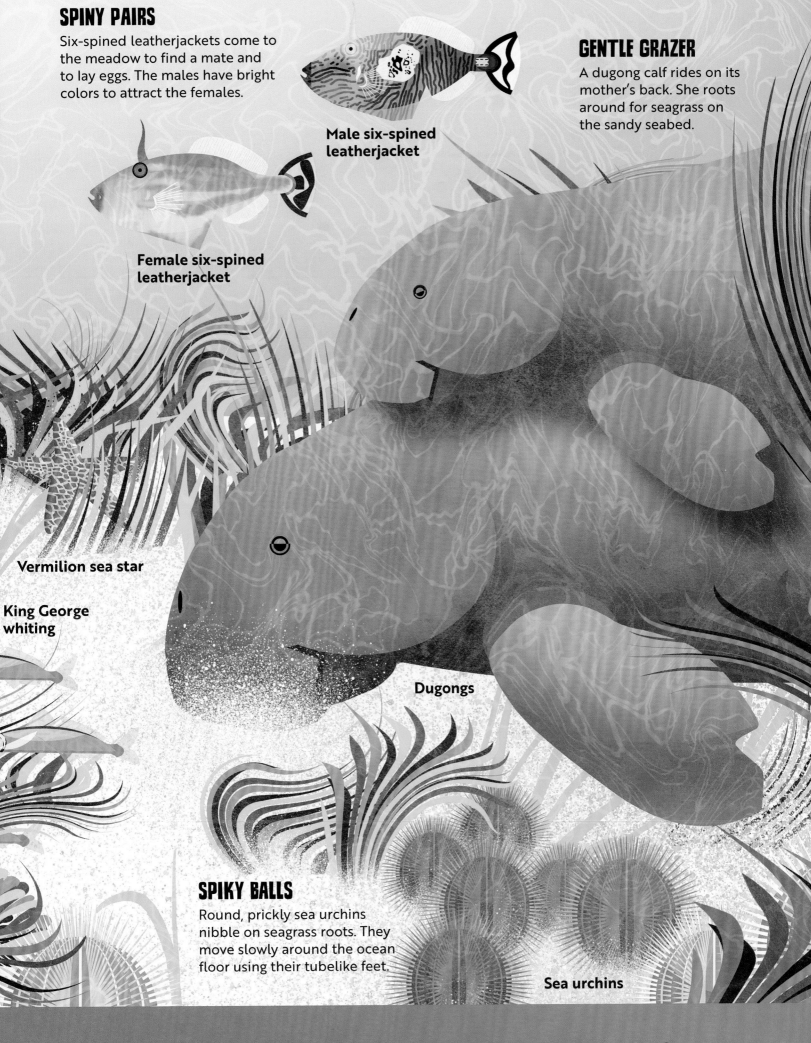

SPINY PAIRS

Six-spined leatherjackets come to the meadow to find a mate and to lay eggs. The males have bright colors to attract the females.

Male six-spined leatherjacket

Female six-spined leatherjacket

GENTLE GRAZER

A dugong calf rides on its mother's back. She roots around for seagrass on the sandy seabed.

Vermilion sea star

King George whiting

Dugongs

SPIKY BALLS

Round, prickly sea urchins nibble on seagrass roots. They move slowly around the ocean floor using their tubelike feet.

Sea urchins

Can you spot a creature that is blue and one that is orange?

UNDERWATER GARDEN

Near the shore is a tangle of giant swaying weeds called kelp. Long stems of kelp stretch up toward the sunny surface of the ocean. Some are as tall as a house!

Lots of different ocean creatures live in this shallow underwater garden. It is a good place to find food or to hide from hungry predators. Some creatures, such as the purple sea urchin, like to feast on the kelp itself. It is easy to spot bright garibaldi fish darting about, but can you see the decorator crab? It covers itself with sponges and seaweed to make a clever disguise.

SWIFT SWIMMER

A California sea lion tumbles and turns as it tries to catch fish. It uses its powerful fins to change direction.

California sea lion

Garibaldi fish

Gray whales

GIANT VISITORS

A large gray whale and her young calf rest between the tall weeds. They are well hidden from predators such as orcas.

DEEP DIVER

A sea otter holds its breath and dives down to the seabed. It is searching for purple sea urchins to eat.

Decorator crab

Sea otter

TOOTHY FISH

The California sheephead has big teeth and strong jaws. It can munch the shells of crunchy crabs.

California sheephead

Purple sea urchins

Rockfish

SPOT IT! How many spiky urchins can you count? Which creatures have whiskers?

Surgeonfish

RAINBOW REEF

The warm, shallow waters of tropical oceans are home to dazzling coral reefs. This sunlit world is alive with colorful sea creatures—and that includes the coral!

Corals are made up of millions of tiny creatures called polyps. They come in many different shapes, such as fans and feathers, and in a rainbow of colors. Corals have hard bodies. When lots of them grow together, they make a rocky reef. Thousands of brightly patterned fish find food and shelter among the reef's nooks and crannies.

Butterfly fish

Butterfly fish

Batfish

Angelfish

BIG BELLY

Pufferfish scare off predators by swelling up to more than twice their normal size. They do this by gulping lots of water.

Pufferfish

Giant moray eel

Damselfish

SNEAKY HUNTER

A fierce giant moray eel peeps out of the reef at night. It is waiting to gobble up passing fish.

Emperor angelfish

SPOT IT! How many clownfish can you see?

CLEANING STATION

Some creatures come to the reef to be cleaned. Little wrasses are eating the dead skin of a big humphead wrasse.

Cleaner wrasse

Humphead wrasse

Hawksbill turtle

POINTED BEAK

Hawksbill turtles have a sharp, pointed beak. They use it to dig out food from between the corals.

Groupers

Cornetfish

Lionfish

Damselfish

Giant clam

Parrotfish

Clownfish

Sea star

Sea anemones

Can you find the cornetfish poking out from the corals?

MEET THE SHARKS

The ocean's top hunters are on the prowl! Sharks live in every ocean and have super senses for finding their food. Most have a long, pointed body that slips smoothly through the water. The biggest fish in the ocean is a shark—the huge whale shark.

Some sharks use their razor-sharp teeth and bone-crunching jaws to snap up their prey. Others simply hold their mouths wide open to catch as many tiny sea creatures as possible.

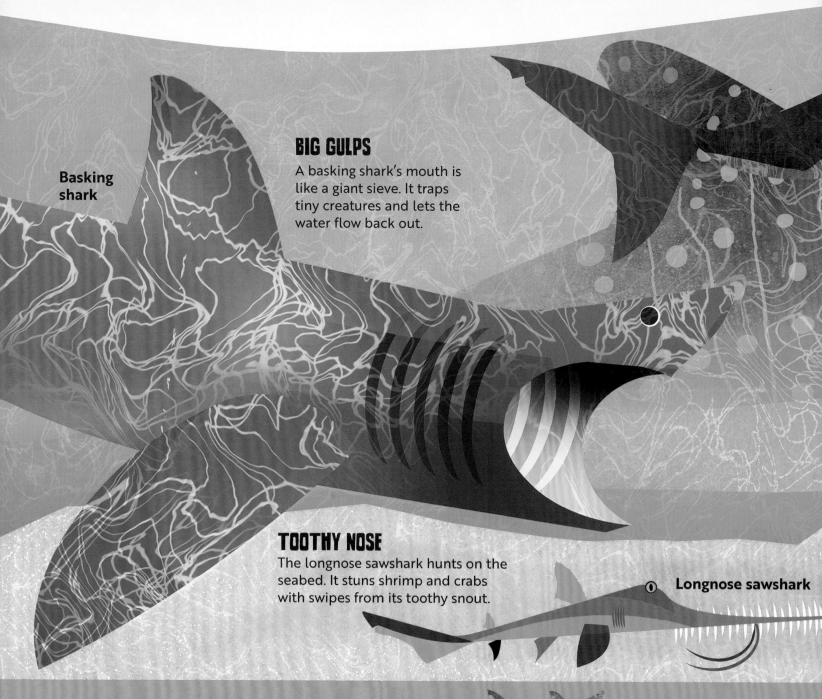

Basking shark

BIG GULPS

A basking shark's mouth is like a giant sieve. It traps tiny creatures and lets the water flow back out.

TOOTHY NOSE

The longnose sawshark hunts on the seabed. It stuns shrimp and crabs with swipes from its toothy snout.

Longnose sawshark

SPOT IT! Which is the heaviest shark?

Basking shark = 1 Asian elephant

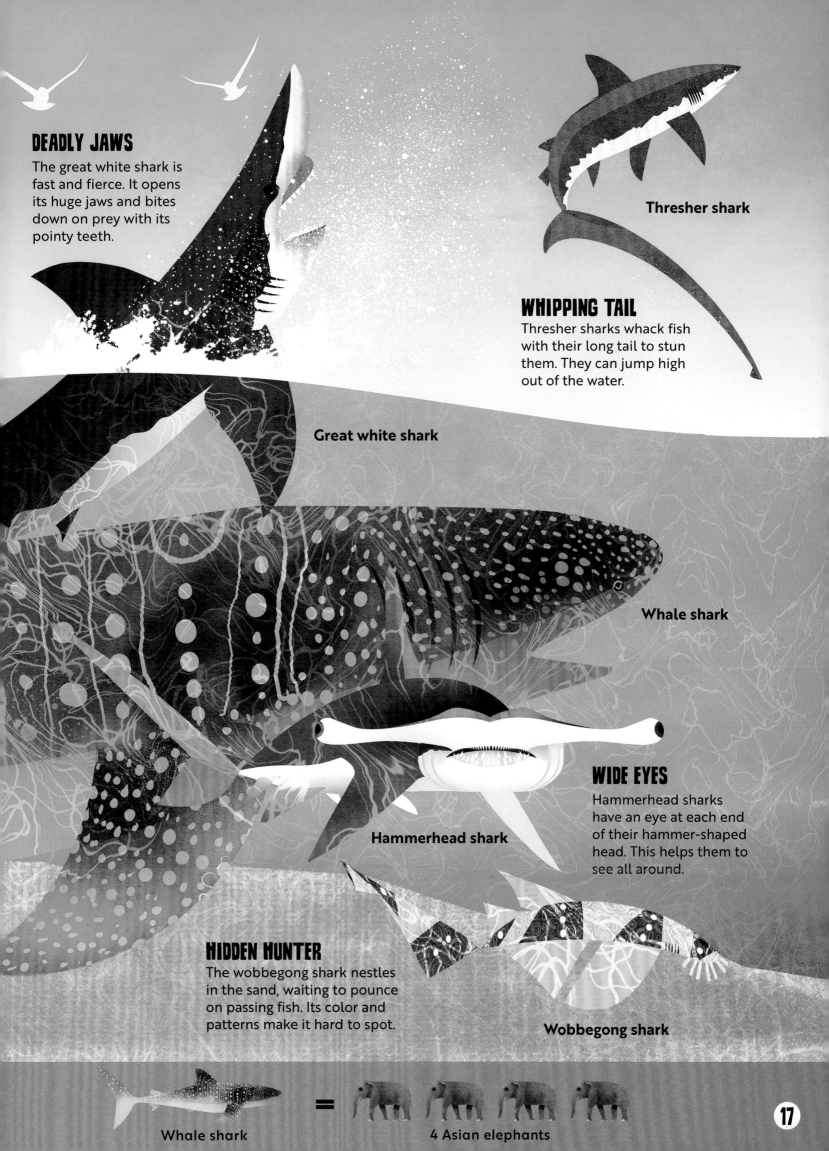

DEADLY JAWS

The great white shark is fast and fierce. It opens its huge jaws and bites down on prey with its pointy teeth.

Thresher shark

WHIPPING TAIL

Thresher sharks whack fish with their long tail to stun them. They can jump high out of the water.

Great white shark

Whale shark

WIDE EYES

Hammerhead sharks have an eye at each end of their hammer-shaped head. This helps them to see all around.

Hammerhead shark

HIDDEN HUNTER

The wobbegong shark nestles in the sand, waiting to pounce on passing fish. Its color and patterns make it hard to spot.

Wobbegong shark

Whale shark = **4 Asian elephants**

THE FROZEN NORTH

Brrr! The Arctic Ocean is a very cold place at the top of the world. In winter, the surface of the ocean freezes and everything is covered in a glistening blanket of snow and ice.

Many creatures live here, despite the cold. To keep themselves warm, seals, walruses, whales, and polar bears have a thick layer of fat called blubber under their skin. They need to be good hunters to catch enough food to eat.

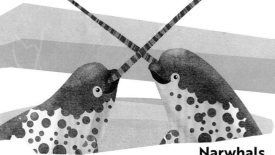

BIG TOOTH

Male narwhals have a pointy, spiral tusk that is actually a long tooth. They are called the unicorns of the sea but they are really a type of whale.

Narwhals

STRONG SWIMMER

Polar bears live on the ice, but they can spend all day hunting for seals in the freezing ocean. They use their paws like paddles to power through the water.

Polar bear

SPOT IT! How many types of creatures have tusks?

Kittywakes

HEAVY BODIES

Walruses are big and blubbery. They wriggle along slowly on the ice, then flop into the water to search for food.

SPECIAL FEELERS

A bearded seal pops up to take a breath. It uses its long whiskers to feel for crabs on the ocean floor.

Walruses

Bearded seal

Walrus

DEADLY HUNTER

This orca is looking for its dinner. It has strong jaws for snapping up fish, seals, and walruses.

PALE WHALE

The white beluga whale can stay underwater for about 20 minutes at a time. Then it needs to come up for air.

Beluga whale

Orca

Which creature has claws on its paddle-shaped paws?

GLOW IN THE DARK

Deep down in the ocean, where no sunlight can reach, thousand of tiny lights twinkle and gently glow. These dots of blue light in the darkness are made by lots of strange deep-sea creatures.

Light made by living things is called bioluminescence. Some creatures flash a warning to predators—KEEP AWAY! Others hide in the inky blackness and use their lights to attract their next fishy meal.

SQUID SURPRISE

The vampire squid shakes the shining tips of its arms at predators to give them a shock. It also squirts glow-in-the-dark gloop to distract them.

SHY SHRIMP

The deep-sea shrimp spits out a cloud of glowing goo when threatened. This startles predators and gives the little shrimp time to escape.

Deep-sea shrimp

Vampire squid

YUCKY GUTS

The pink see-through fantasia has a totally clear body. It glows to show off its insides, which puts off hungry hunters.

Pink see-through fantasia

SPOT IT! Which creature has lots of sharp teeth?

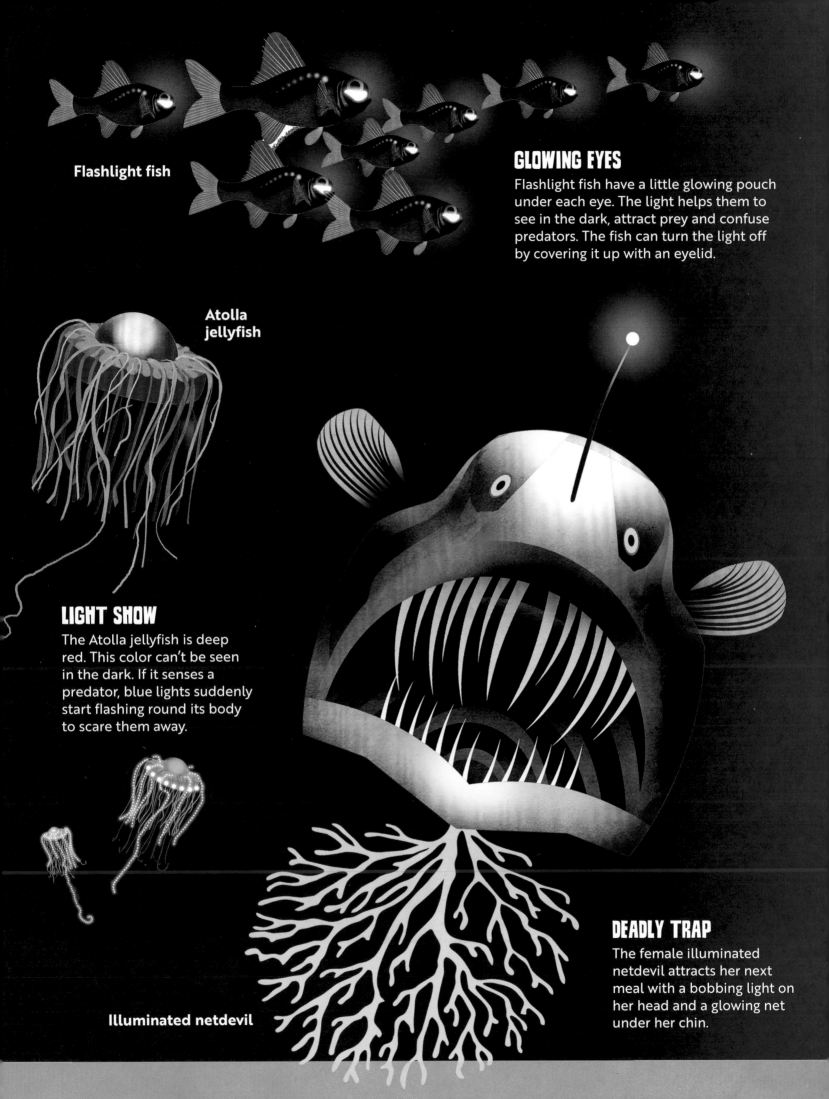

Flashlight fish

GLOWING EYES

Flashlight fish have a little glowing pouch under each eye. The light helps them to see in the dark, attract prey and confuse predators. The fish can turn the light off by covering it up with an eyelid.

Atolla jellyfish

LIGHT SHOW

The Atolla jellyfish is deep red. This color can't be seen in the dark. If it senses a predator, blue lights suddenly start flashing round its body to scare them away.

Illuminated netdevil

DEADLY TRAP

The female illuminated netdevil attracts her next meal with a bobbing light on her head and a glowing net under her chin.

How many flashlight fish are there? Which creature is see-through?

PLUCKY PENGUINS

At the bottom of the world is an icy land called Antarctica. It is the coldest and windiest place on Earth. No trees or plants grow here, but the ocean around Antarctica is rich with life and full of activity.

Boisterous Adélie penguins dive and dart about as they hunt for food and boldly fend off predators. These little birds can't fly, and they waddle awkwardly when they walk, but they are super swimmers. They spend most of their lives in the cold water.

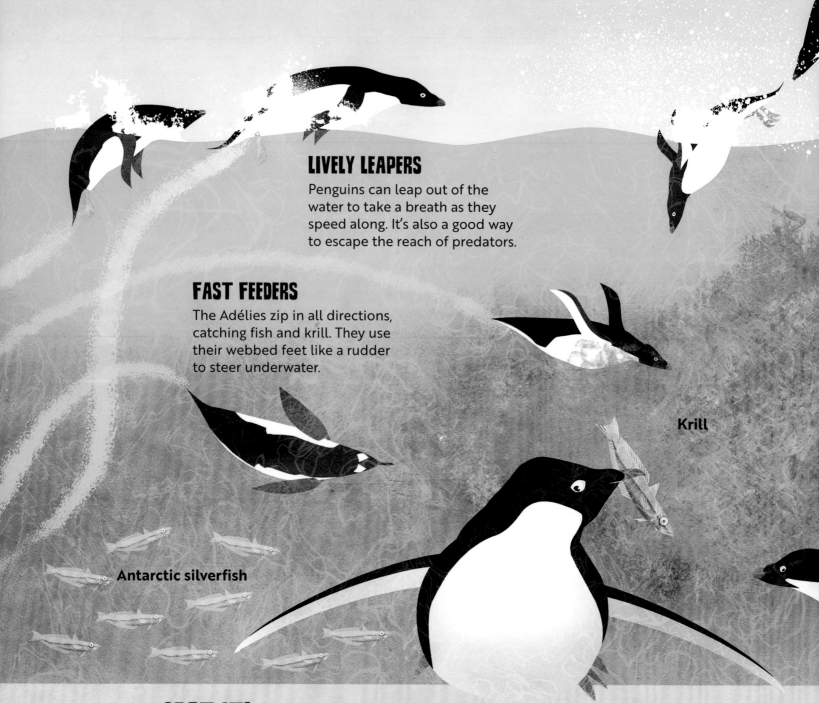

LIVELY LEAPERS
Penguins can leap out of the water to take a breath as they speed along. It's also a good way to escape the reach of predators.

FAST FEEDERS
The Adélies zip in all directions, catching fish and krill. They use their webbed feet like a rudder to steer underwater.

Krill

Antarctic silverfish

SPOT IT! How many penguins are diving into the water?

HIGH DIVERS

Adélie penguins shuffle to the edge of the ice, then dive into the water. They can plunge down hundreds of yards before bobbing up again for air.

Adélie penguins

TUMMY SLIDERS

Penguins can slither over the smooth ice on their bellies, pushing themselves along with their feet. It's quicker and less tiring than waddling.

FAVORITE FOOD

Krill are little shrimplike creatures that drift around in the ocean. They are packed with goodness for penguins.

HIDDEN DANGER

A leopard seal waits for the Adélies to dive into the water. This fierce hunter has huge jaws and sharp teeth to snap one of them up.

Leopard seal

What are the trails in the water made from?

SMOKING CHIMNEYS

All the way down at the bottom of the ocean, dark clouds pour from chimneys on the seabed. This is not smoke, but very hot water gushing out from holes called vents. The cloudy liquid carries material from deep underground. Slowly, this material collects around the holes and forms chimneys. These are known as smokers. Underwater chimneys can grow as tall as a high-rise building!

Strange creatures make their homes around smoking chimneys. There are feathery worms and snails with frilly feet. Hairy crabs cling to the rocks, and ghostly pale fish search for food in the darkness.

HOT SPOT

Scalding-hot seawater shoots out of the vents. It has been heated by volcanoes below the seabed.

WARM EGGS

Deep-sea skates lay their eggs near a chimney. The hot water keeps the eggs warm. This means the eggs hatch more quickly.

Pompeii worm

Vent ratfish

Deep-sea skate

TINY TEAM

It looks like a fuzzy flower, but a sea dandelion is a group of tiny creatures. The creatures all work together to find food.

Sea dandelion

BIG EATERS

Zoarcid fish move slowly and eat steadily. They gobble up anything from tube worms to crabs.

Zoarcid fish

Giant tube worms

TALL TUBES

Giant tube worms poke feathery red gills out of their hard tube bodies. They can pull the gills back in if they sense danger.

Yeti crabs

Feather duster worms

Skate eggs

Scalyfoot snail

SNEAKY SNACKER

A vent octopus creeps out of its hidey-hole. It is looking for crabs and little shrimplike creatures to eat.

Vent octopus

MINI MONSTERS

Yeti crabs are white and hairy. They climb on top of each other to get as close to the chimney as possible.

Squat lobsters

Deep-sea mussels

SPOT IT! Can you find three different kinds of worm? Which creatures have claws?

OCEAN GIANTS

Meet the ocean's record breakers! Whales are the biggest creatures on Earth, and the blue whale tops them all. This gentle giant is the largest creature ever to have existed—it's as long as an airplane! The sperm whale wins the prize for the biggest brain—it's six times the weight of a human brain.

Some of the largest creatures of their kind live in the coldest and deepest parts of the ocean. These mysterious giants are rarely seen. Prepare to be amazed!

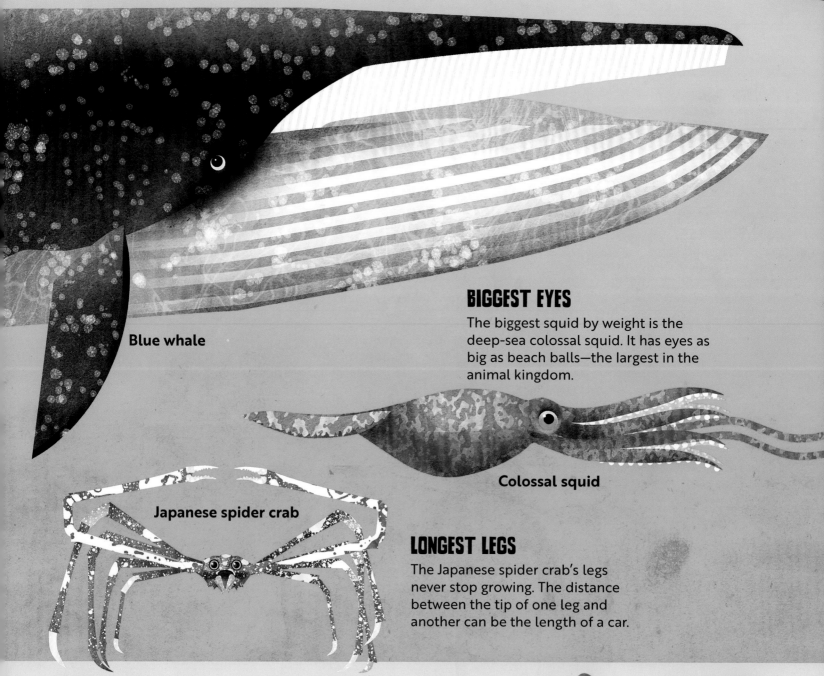

Blue whale

BIGGEST EYES

The biggest squid by weight is the deep-sea colossal squid. It has eyes as big as beach balls—the largest in the animal kingdom.

Colossal squid

Japanese spider crab

LONGEST LEGS

The Japanese spider crab's legs never stop growing. The distance between the tip of one leg and another can be the length of a car.

SPOT IT! Can you order these ocean giants by length, starting with the shortest?

 120 ft.

 50 ft.

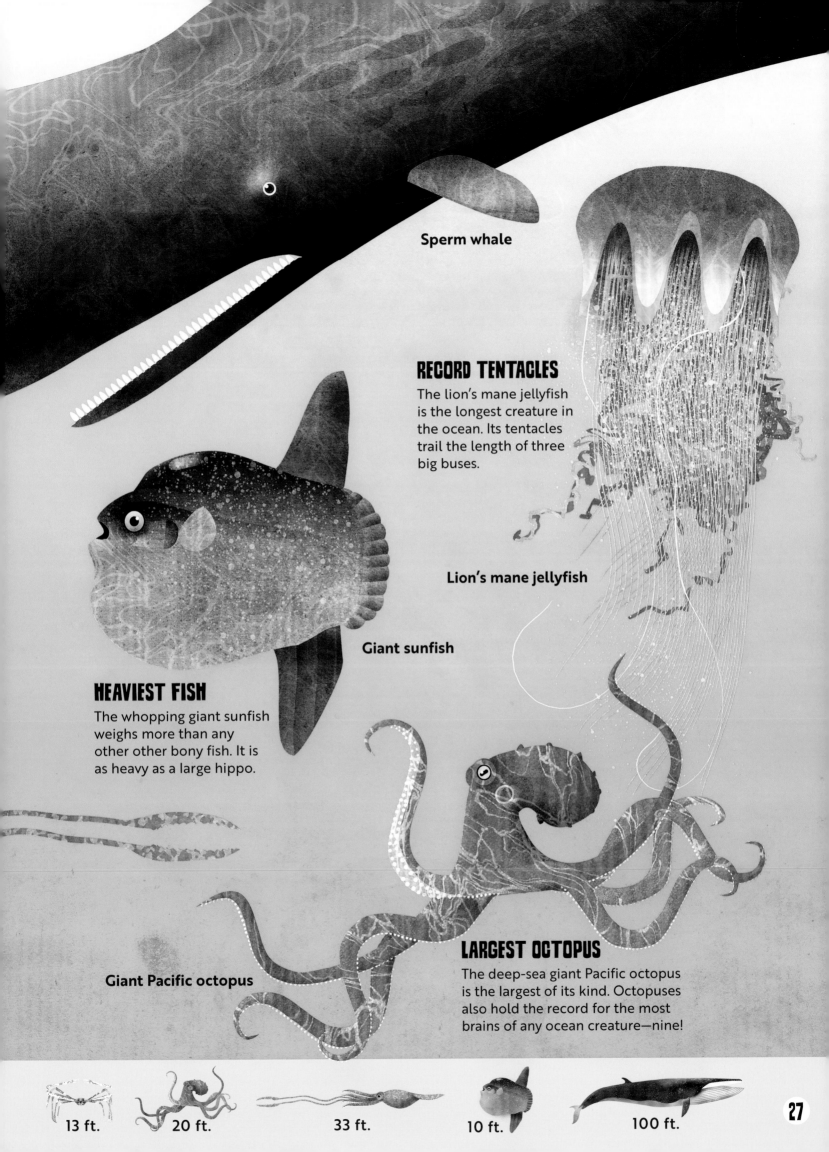

Sperm whale

RECORD TENTACLES

The lion's mane jellyfish is the longest creature in the ocean. Its tentacles trail the length of three big buses.

Lion's mane jellyfish

Giant sunfish

HEAVIEST FISH

The whopping giant sunfish weighs more than any other other bony fish. It is as heavy as a large hippo.

LARGEST OCTOPUS

The deep-sea giant Pacific octopus is the largest of its kind. Octopuses also hold the record for the most brains of any ocean creature—nine!

Giant Pacific octopus

13 ft. 20 ft. 33 ft. 10 ft. 100 ft.

DINNERTIME!

The water flashes with thousands of shimmering fish. It's a giant school of sardines! They have attracted the attention of lots of other creatures, who are looking for their next meal.

There is nowhere to hide in the open seas. The sardines try to stay safe by packing themselves tightly into a swimming swarm called a bait ball. But the clever ocean predators use their amazing skills to make sure they don't go hungry.

NOSE DIVE

A flock of Cape gannets spots a lot of fish near the surface. They fold their wings and dive in to snap them up.

Cape gannets

GOOD TEAMWORK

Common dolphins travel in large groups. They work together to herd the fish close to the surface so that they can't escape.

Common dolphin

WHISKERY SEALS

Cape fur seals have good eyesight, but their sensitive whiskers help them to find fish even when the water is churned up.

Cape fur seal

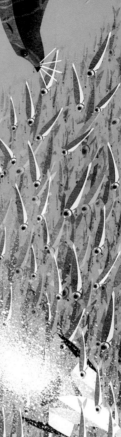

28

DARTING TUNA

Black skipjack tuna are powerful swimmers. They dash in and out of the bait ball, changing direction in a split second.

Black skipjack tuna

SLIPPERY SHARKS

With their pointed noses and smooth bodies, copper sharks speed easily through water to be a part of the action.

Copper shark

MONSTER MOUTH

Last to arrive is a Bryde's whale. It scoops up thousands of fish in one gigantic gulp. The water whooshes out again, but the fish are left behind to be swallowed whole.

Bryde's whale

SPOT IT!

How many gannets can you see? What is the swarm of fish called?

OCEAN WORDS

ANTARCTICA—the area at the bottom of the world around the South Pole. It is almost completely covered in ice. Five different kinds of penguin live in Antarctica, including the Adélie penguin.

ARCTIC OCEAN—the water that surrounds the Arctic. This is the icy area at the top of our planet where the North Pole lies.

BAIT BALL—the name for a school of fish that packs itself tightly into a round shape. It is harder for **predators** to catch the ones in the middle of the ball.

BIOLUMINESCENCE—light created by the body of a living creature. Many jellyfish and deep-sea creatures are bioluminescent.

BLUBBER—the thick layer of fat under the skin of ocean creatures such as whales and seals. Blubber keeps creatures warm in freezing-cold temperatures.

CHIMNEY—a tall pipe that forms around a **vent**, or hole, in the ocean floor.

COAST—where the land meets the ocean.
See also **Shore**.

CORAL—a creature made of thousands of **polyps**. The soft polyps can make a hard body to keep themselves safe from **predators**. Corals live together in groups called colonies.

CORAL REEF—an area where lots of **coral** colonies grow close together. They are usually found in warm, shallow waters. Coral reefs provide food and homes for many different sea creatures.

CREVICE—a narrow crack or gap in or between rocks.

CURRENT—the steady movement of water in one direction.

FIN—a flat part that sticks out of the body of a fish. Most fish have five to seven fins. They help fish to swim and keep their balance.

GILLS—the slits on the sides of a fish that it uses to breathe.

KELP—a big, brown plant, or seaweed, found underneath the surface of the ocean. Kelp plants have a long stem called a stipe and bladelike leaves.

KELP FOREST—an area in cool, shallow water close to the shore where a lot of **kelp** grows close together.

MANGROVE—a **tropical** tree that grows in seawater. Its roots grow up out of the ground to keep the rest of the tree dry.

MANGROVE FOREST—an area on **tropical coasts** where lots of **mangrove** trees grow together. Mangrove forests are often found where a river meets the ocean.

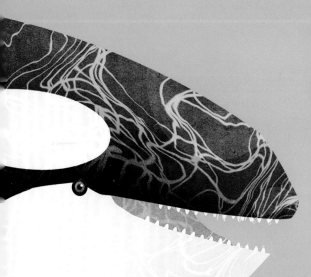

POLYP—a small, tube-shaped water creature. It has a mouth and stinging **tentacles**. It can live on its own like a **sea anemone** or with lots of others in a coral.

PREDATOR—an animal that hunts, kills, and eats other animals.

PREY—an animal that is hunted and eaten by another animal.

REPTILE—an animal, such as a turtle or snake, that has scaly skin and lays eggs. Reptiles need heat from the sun to keep their bodies warm.

SEA ANEMONE—a soft, brightly colored sea creature with stinging **tentacles**. Anemones often live on rocks.

SEAGRASS—a plant that looks like grass that grows in shallow waters near to the **shore**.

SEAGRASS MEADOW—a large area of **seagrass**. These meadows help to keep the ocean healthy. They are home to lots of fish, sea turtles, and **urchins**.

SENSES—the name for sight, hearing, smell, touch, and taste.

SHORE—the narrow strip of land beside an ocean or river. *See also* **Coast**.

SNOUT—an animal's nose.

TENTACLES—long, thin parts of creatures such as jellyfish and **sea anemones**. They are used to touch, taste, smell, hold, and sting other things.

TIDE—the rise and fall of the ocean twice every day.

TIDE POOL—a shallow pool of seawater that is left on the rocky **shore** when the **tide** goes out.

TROPICAL—things from the tropics. The tropics are areas around the middle of the Earth where it is warm all year.

URCHIN—a round sea creature that is covered in sharp spines. Urchins are often found in **seagrass meadows** and **kelp forests**.

VENT—an opening in the ocean floor. Huge **chimneys** often form above them.

A–Z OF OCEAN CREATURES